ALONE BUT NOT LONELY

Alone But Not Lonely

✳

One Woman's Hike on Vermont's Long Trail

Annie Gibavic

BONDCLIFF BOOKS
LITTLETON, NEW HAMPSHIRE

Alone But Not Lonely by Annie Gibavic

Copyright © 2003 by Anne Gibavic

Library of Congress Card Number: 2003103757
ISBN 1-931271-07-0

All rights reserved. No part of this book may be reproduced in any form or by any electronic or mechanical means including storage and retrieval systems without permission in writing from the publisher, except by a reviewer who may quote brief passages.

Text composition by Passumpsic Publishing, St. Johnsbury, Vt.

Printed in the United States by Sherwin Dodge Printers, Littleton, N.H.

Additional copies of this book may be obtained directly from:
  Bondcliff Books
  P.O. Box 385
  Littleton, NH 03561

*Dedicated to my dad,
George Gibavic*

CONTENTS

	Acknowledgments	ix
	Introduction	xi
1	The First Day	1
2	Solitude and Simplicity	8
3	Following Boss Hog	17
4	Fiddler on the Trail	24
5	Mt. Mansfield, Ladders, and Rock Concerts	30
6	Jonesville and the Hump	38
7	General Stark's Palace	45
8	Midway–Middlebury–Snowberry	53
9	A Day on the Trail and More Trail Magic	60
10	The Inn at Long Trail and Sunset on Killington	65
11	Peaks and Lakes	72
12	A Day for the Dogs	78
13	Massachusetts	83
14	Re-Entry	91
	Afterword	95

ACKNOWLEDGMENTS

I would like to thank my mom, Annette Gibavic, for encouragement and editing, as well as for saving and sharing the writings of all my adventurous Vermont ancestors;

...my children, Jamie and Eben, who are diamonds;

...my siblings, and in-laws for encouragement in many forms;

...Wendy, Tune, Suzanne, and Parsh, for sharing life and hikes;

...the people of the Northeast Kingdom, for their diversity, stubborn independence, and acceptance of those who choose a variety of trails and pathways;

...and most of all my husband, Bill, for helping to make so many of my dreams come true.

INTRODUCTION

I hiked the Long Trail in the summer of 2000—270 miles from Canada to the Massachusetts border, over the spine of the Green Mountains of Vermont. It was a trip I had dreamed about for a long time. My resolution in the year 2000 was to do some of the things I had talked about, so there I was, 47 years old, with a pack on my back, heading south.

Sitting on my porch swing after the hike was over, I began to slowly make the transition back to my "real world." Resting my feet and readjusting my mind, I began to read whatever I could find on hiking in general and the Long Trail in particular. Personal accounts, with the shared and differing thoughts and reactions of other hikers, were the most rewarding. Although there are many accounts of the Appalachian Trail, stories of the Long Trail were hard to find. So I started writing my own stories. I found that writing put a part of me back in the woods, placing one foot in front of the other along the trail.

My hope is that this tale will be satisfying to others during that transition time, and inspire those who think "maybe some day" to take three weeks and hike over the tops of the Green Mountains of Vermont.

ALONE BUT NOT LONELY

1

The First Day

What an amazing mix of emotions filtered through the excitement as we headed to North Troy to begin my journey. Joy was the first when I awoke early to a clear morning. The sun was just peeking over the horizon and into my bedroom window. A clear day is always a good omen, especially for hikers. Next came the thought that this was the last time I would sleep in a bed for awhile. A wave of melancholy emerged as I kissed my sleeping sons goodbye. I was already missing them as my husband, Bill, and I left the driveway. Then goodbye and good luck to the garden, where I would usually be enjoying coffee at this time of day.

As we drove north on Route 105, Jay Peak loomed into sight, sending waves of anticipation through me.

Starting out from the U.S.-Canada border at North Troy.

This would be my first big climb, and my tentative goal for the day. I got out my guidebook to find the way to the trailhead. I remember thinking that it was a long way from North Troy to Journey's End Camp. How did folks hiking north get rides at the end of their hike? As we parked the car, the journey started to become real, and again nerves and anticipation mixed with excitement.

Bill and I walked the 1.3 miles from the parking lot to mile marker 592 on the Canadian border, officially the end of the Long Trail. I had decided to hike the trail "backwards" for a few reasons. As I live within an hour of the Canadian border, it was easy to transport me to the northern end. The main reason, however, was that psychologically for me it is downhill to Massachusetts, so to hike "up" the state of Vermont seemed like a much more difficult journey.

In actuality, the trail at the southern border has a slightly higher elevation than up north. The more challenging hiking is on the north and central part of the LT. It is also more isolated. Some people like to start off relatively easy, and work their way into shape for the tough, northern peaks. In most tasks, I would rather get the difficult part over with first. So there I was in North Troy, ready to hike south for the next three weeks.

We met a pair of young women as we walked to the trailhead. I was thinking about the weight of the pack I was carrying, wondering if I was too old for this, and if my boots were really broken in enough. Trying to push aside these little doubts, I noticed that the young women were barefoot! They told us that they had finished the trail the day before. Bill jokingly asked if they had hiked the whole trail barefoot. We thought they were joking when they answered, "Yes!"

We looked at their feet, which were muddy, but appeared to be in great shape (much better than mine were at the end of my hike). The whole interchange was a boost for me. It brought back the spirit of adventure, of being young and carefree, and I remember thinking that if they could hike the trail barefoot, surely I could do it with boots on. During the next few days, I would smile each time I saw "bare" footprints in the mud, and their spirit would lighten my load.

The cleared swath which marks the United States border is quite dramatic at mile marker 592, allowing a view into the Canadian wilderness. The sun was still shining, and the day was warming. After photos and goodbyes, I was suddenly alone, walking in the woods, following the white slashes I would be looking at for the next three weeks.

Snakes warming themselves on the rocks, partridge families fluttering alarmingly in all directions, and frogs hopping out of my way blended with the summer sounds of insects buzzing and the smells of warm mud and wet woods. I had recently finished choreographing a musical, and songs from the show were blending with the forest sounds, transitioning my life from one of music and song and dance to one of subtler sounds and rhythms.

I purposely had not brought a watch with me, but at some point in the morning I stopped for a snack and water. Sitting on a rock looking at Jay Peak still a distance away, I decided to get my bearings. Reaching into my pack, I discovered that my Long Trail guidebook was not where I was sure I had put it. With mounting concern mingling with "Don't Panic," I searched through my entire pack. It wasn't there. The End-to-End Guide, which is meant as a supplement, was all I had.

Now what? The trip was already becoming more adventuresome than I had anticipated. There was no sense in going back. Bill would probably be long gone, even if he had found the book in the car. Again I thought of the long road from Journey's End to North Troy. I didn't want to go back, anyway. It had taken too many years to get to this point.

Studying the End-to-End guide more closely, I realized it contained information about the shelters, road crossings, and water stops along the LT. As long as the trail was well marked, I figured I should be able to make it to Johnson, some 50 miles away, where Bill and I had tentatively planned to meet. The decision made, the panic subsided and the hike continued.

Aside from the barefoot girls, the only people that I saw on the first day were at the Laura Woodward Shelter, just north of Jay Peak. Many of the folks I met during the first few days were almost finished with their journey. It made my hike seem longer, in a way, to meet folks who were completing the trail, and meeting very few people heading south. Everyone was friendly and encouraging, however, and often gave me a boost when I needed it. Deciding to try for my goal of Jay Peak, I hiked on.

The End-to-End Guide mentioned a swimming spot near the summit, and even though the sun had given way to clouds and some sprinkles, I found the pond and dove in. There is nothing like a swim after a long day of hiking! A snack of late wild strawberries on the ski slope, the returning of the sun, and a beautiful array of blue flag iris and paintbrushes led the way to the peak. I had reached my first goal.

There is supposed to be water on top of Jay Peak, and I am sure there is plenty during the day, when the tramway brings visitors to take in the view the easy way. But the tourists were gone for the day, and I couldn't find the water source. The exhilaration of making my goal was mixed with the need to get closer to water. Should I hike back down to the pond, make the small amount I had last for the night, or continue on?

This was the second time on my first day I considered back-tracking. It wouldn't be the last time on my hike that turning around seemed like it might be the thing to do. In every situation, however, the urge to keep going would take over. I knew I had enough water to last until morning if I didn't cook, which was fine with me. So after enjoying the spectacular view in the late afternoon sun, I started down the mountain. Jay Camp is on the south side of Jay Peak, and I knew there would be water there.

As darkness approached, I no longer cared about water. All I wanted to do was set up my tent and lie down. I was tired, to say the least. It seemed a very long time since I had left my home at sunrise. Jay Camp would have to wait until morning. Climbing into my sleeping bag, I started to shiver. The weather wasn't particularly cold; I guess it was a reaction to the excitement, the sweat and exhaustion, and perhaps a little dehydration.

The shivers were soon replaced with the warmth of satisfaction. I was on my way to completing a 20-year goal, and I had made it through my first day on the trail.

2

Solitude and Simplicity

I had never planned to hike the Long Trail by myself. It was something I had hoped to do with my family as soon as everyone was old enough to carry their own packs. My husband and I would talk about it while carrying babies in backpacks up mountains . . . someday. However, as the kids grew and developed their own lives, it became evident that although they both enjoyed backpacking, three weeks on the trail as a family would take up more of their summer than they wanted to give.

Thoughts of finding another hiking partner, or waiting until the kids were older so Bill and I could go together, milled around in my brain with the realization that solo hiking meant being responsible only for myself. After 20 years of caring for kids, house, garden, and animals, the thought of not having to constantly consider the needs of others did have a certain appeal.

For several years I had worked as the choreographer for a summer children's theater, culminating in August productions each year. In the summer of 2000, the show dates were in July, which meant August was free. My older son had graduated from high school, my younger son had finished eighth grade, Bill had turned 50. It was a summer of change. It was time to hike the Long Trail.

Once my decision was made, Bill and my younger son decided to join me for part of the hike, which would also simplify the food drop situation. Vermont is roughly divided into three sections by Route 2 and Route 4, east-west highways which divide the state, and which are major stopping points for hikers. The post office at Jonesville on Route 2, and the Inn at Long Trail on Route 4, are spots where mail and food can be sent or picked up. Many hikers use these places to replenish their supplies. We decided that Bill would join me at Route 2, bringing my second load of supplies, and hike with me to Route 4, approximately 89 miles, or a third of the trail. When he was picked up I would get my final provisions.

Simplicity was one of the goals of this trip. Many people who hike the trail, and many hikers in general, are much more knowledgeable than I about equipment. Pack weight is always a concern, and I knew from prior experience that 35–40 lbs. was a good load for me.

Living the simple life in a tent tucked neatly in amongst the ferns and birch trees.

Although the Long Trail is set up with shelters more or less within a day's hike of each other, my decision to carry a tent came about because I wanted the flexibility to camp where and when I wanted, regardless of weather and shelter availability.

I grew to really love my tent. Aside from crowded shelters, and reaching shelters at odd times of the day, I found that solitude was another goal of my trip. At the end of a long day of hiking, the ritual of setting up my tent, cooking my meal, writing in my journal, curling up in my sleeping bag and reading until I fell asleep was more satisfying than meeting new people and working out the social responsibilities of spending the night together in a small space.

More than once I set up the tent in the rain, glad that it only took a few minutes. The steam from my soup would take the chill out of the tent and me, and my sleeping bag, which I always kept in a waterproof stuff sack and a garbage bag, would feel absolutely luxurious.

My list of equipment was basic, but I really felt I had what I needed. I had been slowly collecting things for years, the only new purchase for the trip was a pair of L.L. Bean Gore-Tex hiking boots. I usually hike in sneakers, but soggy shoes are no fun, and I thought I might want a little more support. I felt very extravagant when I met the barefoot girls!

Here is my equipment list:

L.L. Bean exterior frame pack
L.L. Bean 1–2 person light stuff tent
L.L. Bean 20° down sleeping bag
L.L. Bean Gore-Tex hiking boots
Gore-Tex raincoat
Alcohol stove and quart of alcohol
Tarp/poncho
One spoon (I started with a fork also, but it kept jabbing me.)
Swiss army knife
One metal cup
2-cup cooking pot
1-cup coffee maker
Flashlight

Peppermint soap
1 novel (*Grapes of Wrath* by John Steinbeck)
1 disposable camera
First aid kit, including bandages, antibacterial ointment, aspirin, and an Ace bandage
Clothes: 1 pair of long pants
          1 pair of shorts
          2 T-shirts
          1 lightweight hooded sweat shirt
          4 pairs of socks
          1 polar fleece vest
Food: (This varied a little during the hike, but not too much)
          Instant oatmeal
          Dry cereal
          Powdered milk
          Coffee (Green Mountain, of course!)
          Trail mix
          Lipton instant dinners
          Ramen soup
          Beef jerky
          Dried fruit
          Cheese
Oh, yes, and I did bring a toothbrush!

It was a wonderful feeling in our world of Wal-Mart mentality to reaffirm how little a person really needs. In my real world I have chosen to live a relatively simple lifestyle. This hike was a step beyond, bringing me back to the day 25 years ago when Bill and I walked into a

A typical overnight shelter on the Long Trail.

grown-over field and decided to build a house with an axe and a bow saw.

People asked before and after the hike, "Didn't you get lonely?" Although I missed my family, and was very excited when they joined me so that I could share the experience, I have to say I was never lonely. One day I was homesick. It was a warm day, and the trail passed through some fields. I realized that I missed being in my garden, which is in the middle of a field.

Later that same day the trail wound above Spring Lake, and I could hear the sounds of children playing in the water. I was hot, and wanted to be at Willoughby Lake, a few miles from my home, where I try to spend part of every day in the summer. However, the feelings passed, and I knew I would be in my garden and at Willoughby soon, probably wishing I was still on the trail. So I focused again on the enjoyment of the moment.

"Weren't you afraid?" was another question nearly everyone asked. "Did you have a cell phone, or mace, or a gun?"

"Afraid of what?" I would always ask in return. Animals, getting hurt, and other people were the three things people mentioned the most. Here are my thoughts on these three concerns.

The biggest animals that live near the Long Trail are moose, black bear and (some say) the catamount. As catamount sightings are extremely rare and questionable, I would have welcomed a look at one, as long as it wasn't too close. I have encountered a mother bear with cubs on my driveway, and once a moose ran straight at me in my garden, stopping short about 20 feet away. I love seeing wildlife, and hoped to see some, but despite huge amounts of moose droppings, the biggest animal I saw on the trail was a partridge.

The animals to be most aware of on the LT—mice and porcupines—are not life-threatening, but can be destructive. Mice are residents at many of the shelters, and porcupines crave the salt that is always present on sweaty packs and boots. Hanging your food, and your pack, if porcupines are in evidence, is a good idea in all of the shelters. When I tented I put my pack in my tent, my boots just outside, and never had a problem.

Becoming injured is a more realistic consideration, especially for solo hikers. Although the LT isn't really crowded, it is a well-established trail, and many people hike it. There was only one day when I saw no one else. As I was hiking south, and most people travel north, I passed folks fairly frequently. The most important aspect of not getting hurt is being careful. But it is easy to turn an ankle while wearing a heavy pack on tired legs. It really comes down to trusting one's own ability to deal with something if it happens, or trusting that some helpful person will happen along if you really need help. Aside from a blister on one heel, luckily, I was accident free.

Realistically, there have been a few cases in which people bothered other people on the LT. Since I began writing this book, a solo woman hiker was murdered in the White Mountains of New Hampshire, not very far away. Most incidents that I have heard of on the LT took place near road crossings, involving people with cars. Hikers don't have much to steal, and aside from the road crossings there isn't much access to the trail. The guidebook specified a few shelters where people have had some trouble, and I made sure I passed those during daylight hours.

For myself, I was cautious and aware at road crossings, and always pitched my tent out of sight of the trail. But I didn't feel afraid. I have to say that everyone I met on the trail was pleasant, and was out there to enjoy the same things as I—simplicity and solitude.

3

Following Boss Hog

Interesting relationships develop while hiking long distance trails. For those folks traveling at about the same speed in the same direction, and oftentimes ending up at the same shelter in the evening, a friendly camaraderie and sometimes lasting friendship develops. At other times the urge for solitude encourages speeding up or slowing down to get ahead or behind other groups of hikers. Almost all Appalachian Trail hikers and most of the LT thru-hikers travel south to north. For those few who choose to hike the Long Trail "backwards," staying away from other hikers is usually not a problem, but the opportunity to hike with other folks is often not a possibility.

Another sort of relationship that forms involves the

log books, which are kept in each shelter along the trail. Although no one is required to write in these journals, most people at least sign in as a safety precaution. Many folks go much further. Often there are notes to travelers who will arrive soon, or maybe information on such things as trees blocking the way, or bee nests on the trail. Hikers will often make mention, too, of extra nice places to stay if someone is heading to town for the night. They'll also write poems, draw pictures, or give personal essays about their day, the state of the trail or the state of the world. It is all wonderful reading during a lunch break or at the end of a long day.

The majority of hikers use a trail name, the anonymity giving them an extra feeling of freedom and openness. Some names are given by other hikers, some are chosen and some evolve. "Tanny" is a nickname that Bill gave to me after we were stranded in a snowstorm at a college and watched Dr. Zhivago twice in a row. (The name began as "Tanya" and evolved.)

When I first signed in at the Journey's End trailhead, I decided to use Tanny as my trail name. Over the first several days, when I was adjusting to the weight of the pack and trail life in general, I felt as though I was moving very slowly. At one point I was climbing up a steep spot, tripped over a root, and landed on my pack, arms and legs sprawling. A flipped-over turtle was the first image that came to mind. Thus "Tanny the Turtle" was born.

There are many other "turtles" on the trail, as well as "snails," "slugs," and "sloths." I wasn't the only person who felt as though they were creeping along at a snail's pace. I later learned there is a whole group of hikers known as "The Turtles." Slow and steady seemed to describe my method of approaching the trail. I didn't hike fast, but I didn't stop much, and often I would get a second wind in the evening and hike until nearly dark. When my husband and son joined me they took turns doing the "Turtle Watch," waiting for me to catch up, but I was always the first one ready to go in the morning.

When I woke up after my first night on the trail, having hiked about 13 miles the day before, and still in need of water, I knew that I was not far from Jay Camp. I decided to wait and eat after I had found water, so I packed up my tent and was back on the trail. I hiked the side trail into Jay Camp, peeked inside to see someone still asleep, and continued on. My legs were a little stiff but I felt good, and it was another beautiful morning.

After crossing Route 242 at Jay Pass, and filling up my water bottles, I stopped and ate at a pretty spring and then hiked back up to the ridge. Unfortunately, all of the water on the Long Trail is susceptible to impurities. The guidebooks stress purifying the water by either using a filter pump or iodine tablets. I began the hike using iodine, but found the taste really kept me from drinking water. I did drink a good amount of untreated water,

Looking back at Jay Peak from the fire tower
atop Belvidere Mountain.

when I would find a fast flowing stream, which worked very well. (I have heard that adding vitamin C to iodine-treated water helps to dispel the taste, and I would certainly suggest trying it to anyone planning to use iodine for water purification.)

Whenever the Long Trail crosses a road, it usually means a hike downhill to the road and then a hike back up to the ridge. The roads were generally built where a stream cuts through a pass in the mountains, so road crossings often mean water, also. Back on the ridge, and having seen no one all morning, I was startled to hear someone behind me. A younger than me hiker passed by with a hello. Judging by his gear and his hiking speed, I didn't think I would see him again, but I did pass him once more when he took a break. Then he passed me for the last time.

"Boss Hog," I learned from the hiking journals, was planning to hike 15 miles per day. Although I didn't see him again, I would check each trail journal to see how far ahead of me he was. Although my pace was slower, it was reassuring to follow someone else hiking south. At 15 miles per day the Long Trail can be hiked in 18 days. Although the LT discourages speed hiking, and makes no acknowledgement of records for fastest hikes, I am sure "Boss Hog" made, or at least came close to his goal.

Another southbound hiker I did get to meet was "Mitch." I followed the name in the trail logs for some time before a northbound hiker explained that Mitch was another solo woman hiker. I did catch up with her near Camel's Hump; it was fun to meet someone I had been reading about for a week. Bill and I named one group of hikers the "Celery People," after they passed us and left a celery sculpture in the middle of the trail. I don't know if the "Barefoot Girls" was actually a trail name, but everyone on the trail had either met them or heard about them.

One amazing trail reunion I was able to witness was at Birch Glen Camp. My husband, son and I had just hiked over Camel's Hump in the rain, and spent two nights in a two-person tent because of crowded shelters. We bypassed Cowles Cove Shelter, having heard that Birch Glen was much bigger. We hoped it wouldn't be full. Luck was with us. There was only one other person there, and the shelter is one of the biggest on the trail, with a sleeping room and a roofed porch/eating room.

Just at dark another hiker came in, and as we were all cooking our various pasta varieties, we visited about trail conditions and hiking history. As it turned out, one of the men had hiked the Appalachian Trail, and was now finishing the Long Trail. (The LT and AT are the same trail from the Massachusetts border to Killington, Vermont; though just a small part of the AT, this represents about half the length of the Long Trail. Many AT hikers come back to finish the LT.)

As our companion for the evening described his AT hike, the other hiker looked a little closer in the candle light, and said, "Ben?" It turned out that they had both hiked the AT the same year, had hiked a section together, and hadn't seen each other since. One of them was hiking north, the other hiking south, and it was merely coincidence that they had stopped at the same shelter.

They reminisced about other mutual hiking companions, and I felt again the camaraderie of folks who choose to spend their time in the woods. To all those folks who hiked the Long Trail in the year 2000, thank you for your pleasant hellos and for your entries in the journals. For me it was a wonderful way to share the trail.

4

Fiddler on the Trail

During the planning stage of my trip—trying to fit it in between choreographing for the Vermont Children's Theater in July and taking my son to college in late August—I realized that I would be on the trail during the Lamoille County Players' performance dates for "Fiddler on the Roof" in Hyde Park. I had choreographed "Fiddler" the previous winter, and a friend was choreographing for this show, so I really was hoping to attend. Knowing that the trail crosses Route 15 in Johnson (just a few miles from Hyde Park), I made a tentative plan to meet Bill and see the show.

I had no real idea how long it would take me to hike the 50 miles from North Troy to Johnson, so I told him I would call when I got there. I would try for Thursday, but it might be Wednesday or Friday. Aside from losing my guidebook on the first morning, the three days at the beginning of my hike were great. The good weather held, I was getting in shape, and the trail was rugged and beautiful, with incredible views from Jay Peak and Belvidere Mountain.

It rained during my third night out, but had stopped by morning. The woods were magical in the mist. I followed moose tracks to Laraway Lookout, where the fog blew in and out of the view far below. Then it was mostly downhill, the trail winding beneath granite cliffs, and the fog was lifting, allowing for occasional peeks at the sun. Dinner and a show were sounding good.

I arrived at Roundtop Shelter around 1 P.M., according to a man and a rugged 14-year-old who were heading north. They assured me it was all downhill to Johnson, with easy hiking; I should be there in a couple of hours. The sign said 3.6 miles, the sun was coming out. I was envisioning a swim in the Lamoille River, and a burger and beer at the Long Trail Tavern, which is located at the point the trail crosses Route 15.

Arriving at Prospect Rock an hour or so later, the river looked close, and I stretched out in the sun, enjoying the view and giving my feet a rest. When I got back up I looked around a little, as this was obviously a popular spot, with campsites and unmarked side trails, then went back to following the white slashes, the marks of

The view overlooking the Lamoille River from Prospect Rock, 1.7 miles from Route 15 in Johnson.

both the Long Trail and the Appalachian Trail. I started down, but after I had walked awhile the trail seemed to be heading uphill again. Probably climbing to another lookout, I thought.

After what seemed an awfully long time, with the sounds of Route 15 not getting any closer, I saw something through the trees. "Good, it must be a house," I said to myself. "Civilization." But as I got closer it looked rather familiar. It was the outhouse at Roundtop Shelter! No, it couldn't be. It was. I had been heading north since Prospect Rock. I even checked the shelter register, which I had signed a few hours before. There was my name. Two miles of backtracking, two more extra miles to go, and still 3.6 miles to Johnson. By now it must be at least 3 P.M. (Why didn't I bring a watch? Why had I lost my guidebook? Where had I gone wrong? How will I ever get to the show?)

Feeling a little bit stupid and finding it unbelievable that I had recognized nothing on the trail in the last two hours, I did the only thing that made sense to me at that point. I started jogging back down the 3.6 miles to Johnson. Thank goodness it really is almost all downhill and I was feeling like I must be getting in shape. I came to a gravel road I had already crossed twice, and knew that it must go to town. I kept making sure that the traffic sounds were getting closer all the time, and soon houses began to appear, the road improved, and finally I came to Route 15. There was the Tavern; what a welcome sight.

With a glazed or possibly crazed look on my face I found the phone and called my husband. No answer. I checked the time. It was 6:15. I called the theater. The show was at 7:00. "Been hiking?" someone asked. It is amazing how different you feel after just four days of hiking alone in the woods; like from a different planet. I nodded and tried calling Bill again. No answer. Now what? I hadn't done much hitchhiking in about 25 years, but was just asking someone which way they were headed when I heard a voice say, "Can I help you with that pack, ma'am?"

I turned to see my husband, my son, my car. They had decided to take a drive (from Sutton, about 45 minutes away) and see if they could find me. I couldn't believe it. It was my first experience of "trail magic," when what you need is right in front of you. Now 6:45, I threw my pack in the back, then changed my shirt and took off my shoes on the way to Hyde Park. There was no available parking and quite a crowd, so I jumped out (barefoot) to get tickets. Noticing the "sold out" sign in front, the determination and desperation of a few hours earlier kicked in, and I announced to the box office attendant that I had walked from Canada to see this show, and I needed three tickets.

We were able to get tickets and see a great show, although when I got up at intermission I could hardly move. (So much for being in shape!) The three of us camped together that night, and after breakfast and the purchase of a new guidebook in the morning, I went to the Johnson Pharmacy for some Band-Aids. Jogging with a full pack and hiking boots didn't make any sense anymore. There in the pharmacy was another piece of trail magic: a foot massage machine—sit down and try it out for free, said the sign! It was a turning point in my hike, when I realized I really could hike to Massachusetts.

Back on the trail later that afternoon, the hike up

Whiteface Mountain was relaxed and enjoyable. It felt timeless. I had a new guidebook. I was no longer trying to meet anyone or any deadline. My body was strong, and my energy was feeding itself. My mind was along for the ride. Whiteface is a good hike, with a stream nearby. When I arrived at the summit, it was late in the day, and there were some clouds over Lake Champlain. This combination sent shards of sunlight in all directions, silhouetting Mount Mansfield. It was a moment to savor, which I did, along with some fruit leather.

Hiking down is always a mixture of relief and a little letdown, but what goes up must come down, and I soon found myself at Whiteface Shelter, a beautiful spot. I had considered staying there if it was empty, but no such luck, and I was still floating from the day's events, so I kept hiking. Just before dark, the clouds I had seen over Lake Champlain moved in with a little thunder, so I set up camp.

The thunder stayed in the distance, but as it got dark I heard other booming sounds with flashes of light. Fireworks! The Vermont Reggae Festival was taking place that weekend. I remembered meeting two hikers that morning who were heading out to attend. As I drifted off to sleep that night, distant thunder mixed with fireworks and songs of "Fiddler on the Roof," thoughts of the amazing events of the past 24 hours, and excitement about the weeks to come on the Long Trail.

5

Mount Mansfield, Ladders, and Rock Concerts

Mount Mansfield is the highest peak in Vermont, above treeline, and ecologically fragile, due to its popularity and heavy use. Having hiked it before, and knowing that it was the highest point of my hike, I was excited to once again be on top of Vermont. The hike over Madonna Mountain, early in the morning, had been foggy, though I did stop for a few moments at the top of the chairlift of Smuggler's Notch ski area. From the bottom of this lift, on a cold and clear winter's day, the lift seems to go straight up forever. On this day the fog had settled into the notch, with mists rising on the wind currents, an equal but very different kind of beauty.

Crossing over a ski trail on Madonna Peak.

Being alone on top of high peaks is one of my favorite hiking experiences. I had once left my house in the dark to beat the crowd up Mount Mansfield on what turned out to be a spectacular autumn day. This, however, was a Saturday in July, and as I passed crowds of day hikers on their way to Sterling Pond, and walked alongside bumper-to-bumper traffic on the road through Smuggler's Notch, thoughts of solitude were forgotten.

The weather, aside from the rumbles of thunder the night before, had been warm and foggy all morning, with a few peeks at the sun; it was the kind of day that could easily burn off to be really hot. As I walked down the road, an ominous wind and approaching storm clouds promised more thunder and lightning. Halfheartedly looking for a picnic shelter, I thought about the day hikers heading to Sterling Pond, whose clothes might not be so crisp and white on their way back down.

As it became more evident that the clouds would open at any time, I found myself looking at the cars at the trailhead and wondering if anyone would mind if I sat in one until the storm blew over. If there was one thing about the hike of which I was a little apprehensive, it was thunder and lightning storms. I was about to experience my first one, and was glad that it was during the day, and I was on relatively low ground.

I knew that I didn't want to be on Mansfield's unprotected summit during a storm, but I was a few hours away from the peak, and Taft Lodge was en route. So as the skies began to open, I began my ascent. So goes hiking. Here was the thunder and lightning, not to mention torrents of rain, that I had worried about. I was soon drenched, but it was a warm rain, and I didn't bother trying to retrieve my raincoat from the bottom of my pack. Once you are soaked, you don't get any wetter.

The trail became a stream, and lots of people were heading downhill fast. The summit caretakers had cleared the peak, but the suddenness of the storm had caught many people unprepared. These folks would soon be in their cars, with the heaters going full blast, headed to a hot shower and hot chocolate. Some looked at me as though I had really lost my mind.

Madonna Peak (*left*) and Mount Mansfield, Vermont's highest peak, as viewed from the top of Whiteface Mountain.

Quite honestly, I was beginning to wonder myself. I didn't know what I would do if the rain continued. Being a Saturday, I was quite certain that Taft Lodge would be full, and the thought of setting up my tent, on the side of the mountain next to the trail/streambed, was not an exciting one. Taft Lodge appeared, looking secure and dry, a welcome sight indeed.

Surprisingly, there were only a few people inside. The caretakers said there were several groups scheduled to spend the night, but due to the weather, they might or might not show up. The persistent rain and fog were suddenly in my favor. I had been on the trail for six days, and the log walls and rain on the roof reminded me of home. I began to settle in.

There were only six of us in Taft that night, so there was lots of room, as it is the largest shelter on the LT, and has room for 24 people. Another caretaker came to visit, and made grilled cheese sandwiches for everyone, which was a real treat. It was a bit of a party atmosphere for the caretakers, who were used to large crowds, especially on weekends. Butler Lodge, on the other side of Mount Mansfield, was being rebuilt in the summer of 2000, so Taft was even more populated than usual.

Very thankful for a dry night, I awoke early and looked outside. Dense fog had once again settled into Smuggler's Notch, but the sky was blue above, with the summit in clear view. Living on a hill in Vermont, I am very familiar with valley fog, and knew that at some point it would rise. I quickly packed up my still wet clothes from the day before, grabbed a granola bar, and headed up.

For the second time I was alone on top of the highest peak in Vermont on a beautiful morning. The fog was a sea in the valley, but the ridge was mine, quiet in the early morning light. Mount Mansfield from a distance looks like the profile of someone lying on their back, and the peaks are appropriately named the "chin," "nose," and "forehead." I hiked over the chin and the nose, and just as I got to the forehead, the fog began to lift and soon the whole mountain was enveloped.

The forehead of Mansfield is quite steep, with lad-

On the top of Vermont as the valley fog rises far below.

ders and rocks, and I was concerned that it might be slippery from all the rain. Having tentatively set the following day as the next meeting with Bill, when he and my younger son would join the hike, I knew I had to cover a lot of ground. The rain of the day before had shortened my hiking distance considerably. However, this stretch of Mansfield, on a wet morning, is not the place to make good hiking time.

I was glad that it was morning, my favorite time of the day for any sort of challenge. Manipulating the balance of the pack, keeping my footing steady on wet rocks, and moving slowly, the ladders were manageable. I had heard about the difficulty of this section of Mansfield, but had never hiked it, so I experienced a moment of relief when I reached the bottom. From there it was on to Bolton Mountain, the last peak before meeting my hiking partners.

My sons have both ski-raced at Bolton Valley, and compared to some race courses it is not particularly challenging. This impression led me to expect that climbing Bolton Mountain would be a relatively easy hike. After all, I had just finished climbing Vermont's highest peak. This was a wrong assumption; the ski slope is on a different side of the mountain. The day seemed to go on forever; so did the climb. I arrived at Puffer Shelter early in the evening, and was considering stopping if it was empty.

The two gentlemen I found there graciously offered to make room. It was still light, and I thought that if I could get over the top of Bolton, the next day's hike to Jonesville would be mostly downhill. After describing how far I had traveled already, the gentlemen shook their heads at my decision to continue. They had just traveled down the steep backside of Bolton Mountain.

I began counting steps, one of the mindless games I used to keep myself going up steep places. I would count 16 steps, and only allow myself to stop on the count of 16. If I stepped on 1 again, I had to keep going until the next count of 16. I was reminded of a hike down from Tuckerman Ravine in New Hampshire with a tired young child, who counted steps into the thousands. I was regressing.

Exhausted by the time I reached the summit, and watching it grow darker by the minute, I decided to camp at the first available spot. It was that late twilight time when shapes and shadows take on new meaning. I began to imagine cockatiels on the branches, and thought about how much fun it would be to hike where tropical birds were commonplace. Overtired was taking on new meaning.

Suddenly, I began to hear faint music. Thinking exhaustion was getting the best of me, but curious at the same time, I had to keep going. Did someone have a boom box set up at camp? Following switchbacks, I noticed the music grew louder each time I hiked to the left, and softer as I veered to the right. Then I could hear a crowd cheering at the end of a song. I kept hoping the switchbacks would lead to a lookout, but it was really dark at this point in time. I needed to make camp.

As I began setting up my tent, the answer to this puzzle came to me. Each year, various ski areas in Vermont host outdoor concerts on the slopes, which make natural amphitheaters. Ben and Jerry, the ice cream impresarios, helped to establish this tradition with their once a year free-concert-and-ice-cream party. Relieved that my mind was still intact, sleep came quickly amidst the sounds of a cheering crowd and rock and roll.

6

Jonesville and the Hump

"Everything takes longer than you think" sure rang true on the morning after the Bolton Rock Concert. I wasn't sure how far I had to hike to reach Jonesville; I had figured about five miles, but the timelessness of hiking over Whiteface Mountain was gone. I wanted to be in Jonesville immediately. One of the reasons I carried my tent with me on the trail was to never feel as though I had to get somewhere before dark, or had to stop before I was ready. Although I didn't have to be in Jonesville at any particular time, I felt an incredible impatience and urgency. The excitement of sharing the hike with Bill and my son was mounting.

When I looked at my guidebook in Jonesville, I realized I had hiked about nine miles that morning; no wonder it took so long! The trail follows a road under the interstate and into town. I had never been to Jonesville before, although I had traveled over it on Interstate 89 many times. There is no exit or sign on the highway to acknowledge the existence of this small Vermont town like so many others. However, the post office and general store are well known to anyone hiking the Long Trail.

One hiker from the south said that the three-mile road walk south of Jonesville was the hardest part of the trail for him. He felt as though he was in backwoods Vermont and the road gave him blisters. Most hikers dislike the road walk, but enjoy the other benefits of Jonesville.

The P.O. is right on the trail, at the Route 2 road crossing. Approximately two-thirds of the way from Massachusetts, or one-third of the way south, Jonesville is one of the best drop-off spots for supplies. You can mail yourself a package General Delivery before you leave home, and it will be held there for your arrival. The general store, with an outside pay phone, is about a quarter-mile west of the post office.

Bill was meeting me with supplies, so I bypassed the P.O. As I traveled the quarter-mile around the bend to the store, my eyes caught a glimpse of the familiar Green Mountain Coffee sign on the side of the building. (When driving, the beige and green signs will often determine which mini-mart becomes a gas station stop.)

Although I had Green Mountain Coffee in my pack, had given up cream for the hike, and had been drinking almost no coffee, at this moment in my life I really wanted a cup of hazelnut. Hmmm. I wasn't sure if I had any money. It was wonderful not thinking in monetary terms for a week, aside from the stop in Johnson. I realized the few dollars I had carried with me had been spent on the Band-Aids back in Johnson. Then I saw someone eating potato chips. The salt and fat urge was almost as great as the caffeine urge.

The onslaught of civilization in the form of a Vermont general store was upon me. Digging through my pack, I found exactly $1.00 in change, enough for a small cup of coffee and a small bag of chips, and I was one happy camper. Having called Bill, I knew I would have a few hours to wait. I called my parents to let them know I had survived the first leg of my journey. Then sitting down in front of the store, I sipped my coffee, read my book, and waited.

Hikers filtered in and out throughout the afternoon. Folks opened boxes they had received at the P.O., offering to other hikers items they now realized they couldn't use or would just be extra weight. "Anyone want any Power Bars? I've got way too many and I'm sick of them!" Trading food and stories made for an interesting social time.

My seat close to the pay phone allowed me to drift

in and out of eavesdropping while reading. Most folks were excited to have contact with friends and family, although one gentleman complained for about ten minutes straight; something he had sent to the P.O. hadn't arrived, the rain was really bugging him, his knees hurt. Then I overheard him say, "Yes, I'm going to finish, I've gone this far!" It must have been his wife on the other end of the line, I thought, because his manner changed when his hiking partner came out of the store. For some people the challenge becomes more important than the enjoyment.

There is a connection between hikers at Jonesville, made especially evident by the other folks who stop by the store to pick up milk, beer and videos. An alertness and aliveness that comes from being in the woods a long time exudes a different kind of energy than driving in a car. I've certainly had days that were spent almost entirely behind the wheel, and I know the dullness that those days can bring. It felt great to be tired but strong from a lot of physical exercise, and clear from letting my mind go its own way for a week.

After spending a lazy few hours, my husband and son arrived. It was wonderful to see their familiar smiles. My son, an avid reader, was furiously finishing the last chapter of the latest Harry Potter book, and barely said hello. He couldn't stand the idea of being so close to the end but didn't want to carry it with him. It's a big book! A friend had sent a quart of blueberries; her husband was the driver for my hiking partners. I realized that I hadn't spoken much in the last few days, as I tried to detail the hike since seeing them in Johnson. It was a nice visit, and my son was able to finish his book.

It was getting late when we were dropped off at the trailhead. Knowing we wouldn't hike too far that evening, we were nevertheless anxious to get a ways into the woods, so we started off on the trail towards Camel's Hump. My tent is made for 1 to 2 people, but we all snuggled in together that night. We had planned to stay in shelters while the three of us were together, but the timing didn't work out that way on our first night. My son had to keep a journal for an English assignment; I was keeping one also, so we wrote, read, and cuddled. It was nice having company.

We had just finished packing up in the morning when it began to rain, so we ate our oatmeal in a little cave along the side of the trail. It was foggy and rainy all morning, and by the time we arrived at Gorham Lodge, near the top of Camel's Hump, we were ready for hot soup. We debated staying there, but it was early, and we knew that we would have time to get to Montclair Glen Shelter before dark, so we continued. We had decided one night in the tent was cozy, two nights would be cramped.

Camel's Hump is the third highest peak in Vermont,

Eben, left, and Bill pose for a photo atop Burnt Rock Mountain.

and the highest undeveloped summit. I had hiked it before, but my partners hadn't, so I was disappointed that they wouldn't see the spectacular view. There is a bad weather bypass of the summit, and as the wind was blowing the rain sideways and the fog was thick, we decided to use it.

It was a long day of hiking, and we were ready to stretch out on a bunk at Montclair Glen Shelter. Just as we arrived at a little stream near the lodge, we met a large youth group. They said the hut was packed, as well as the tent platforms. Not exciting news for us, but at least the rain had stopped.

There is an unspoken courtesy on the trail that people make room at the shelters, especially for thru-hikers. We thought about trying to work something out, but in the end we set up the tent and cuddled once more. The highlight of the evening was a trade with one of the youth groups. My iodine tablets (Bill had brought a water filter) were exchanged for caramel apples. A sweet treat to top off a dreary day.

7

General Stark's Palace

Everything always looks better in the morning. Despite a little stiffness from the three of us being crowded into a tent for two nights, it was great to have hiking partners and conversation for a change. It quickly became evident, however, that I was the slowest hiker of the trio. My son had brought a harmonica with him, and would sit on a rock and play while he and Bill waited for me to catch up.

The weather was improving, and as we climbed over Burnt Rock Mountain, the fog began to burn off. My husband had brought all kinds of edible treats with him, so we stopped for an elegant lunch of smoked salmon, with wild blueberries for dessert. Quite a change from my usual fare of dried fruit and beef jerky.

For me, one of the joys and satisfactions of hiking is looking back at a ridge and seeing how far I have traveled. During my hike, Jay Peak with its distinguishing notch at the top, was the first milestone. On my first day it loomed ahead, then I was on top of it, then it receded into the distance as I headed south. I would look for it on each summit that afforded a view. Mansfield was my next marker, then Camel's Hump, then Killington. For some folks Glastenbury is the next big peak, but as the weather had deteriorated by the time I passed Killington, I didn't see much except the trail until Massachusetts.

It was disappointing that my son didn't get that feeling of accomplishment looking out from the top of Camel's Hump. However, we live less than two hours from the Hump, so the following October, on a perfect autumn day we took the short route up, and relived a bit of the hike. On that day we could see all the way to Jay Peak in the north, and to Killington in the south, almost the entire length of the Long Trail. It was an inspiring moment for both of us to reflect about our time on the trail.

After a good day of hiking we arrived at Cowles Cove Shelter, empty and inviting. It was still relatively early in the evening, and we had passed hikers who planned to camp at this shelter. We definitely didn't want to spend another night in the tent, but we didn't want to be

Bill and the author stand atop the open summit
of 4006-foot Mt. Abraham.

crowded in a small shelter, either. Birch Glen Camp, another three miles along the trail, was supposed to be bigger, with a better water source.

We let our son decide whether to take the shelter at hand or the one in the bush. He decided to move on, which turned out to be a great decision. The trail headed downhill, and as we hiked, it widened, and flattened through some beautiful hardwoods. It was some of the easiest and most pleasant hiking I had experienced so far.

We came to a very picturesque shelter in the middle of a pretty birch glen, hence the name. A nice stream flows close enough to be heard all night long. There is also a pool downstream deep enough for a quick dip, which, as always, felt wonderful. Best of all, it was almost dark and the shelter was almost empty. There are actual shelf bunks that can accommodate up to twenty people, and since only five of us were spending the night, we could all stretch out luxuriously. Our son would be meeting his grandparents the next day, so along with the reunion of two Appalachian Trail hikers, it felt like a celebratory evening.

Although the next morning was cloudy, it wasn't raining as we hiked up to Appalachian Gap, where Route 17 cuts through the Green Mountains on its way from Waitsfield to Bristol. As we arrived at the road near Mad River Glen Ski Area, the clouds moved in again, with threats of more showers. My son, an avid ski racer, decided that the shortest way to the phone at the ski lodge was down the racing hill. So similar to our skiing patterns in winter, he went straight down and we traversed back and forth across the hill.

Just as we arrived at the sheltered phone, the clouds let go with a downpour. We cooked soup and played cards in the phone shelter, while waiting for our son's ride. We called our message machine, and learned that a friend from college was in Vermont, actually not far from where we would be hiking. It was the one time a cell phone would have been useful, as we had to bypass that reunion.

While we were waiting, Bill went into the ski lodge and found out that the Green Mountain Club and Mad River Glen together had built a new lodge on top of nearby Mount Ellen. It was brand new and had just opened, and would be used in the summer for hikers and in the winter for skiers. We were interested in taking a look at it when we got back on the ridge.

The rain ended just about the time our son's transportation arrived, so we rode into town for a bite to eat and a few supplies. Then our son was packed in the car with his grandparents and visions of a hot bath, a cozy couch and a television. As fog and drizzle moved in once again, my husband and I were back on the trail.

We hiked up the steep pitch towards the ridge, and passed a very small and very full Theron Dean Shelter. Once again it was getting late and raining, so we had considered using a shelter. The folks at Theron Dean mentioned the new building at the top of the ski lift. They called it "The Palace," said it was open, but didn't know any more about it.

The extra push at dusk was worth it. We arrived just before dark at The Palace, complete with a deck, a fireplace and enough floor space, no, carpet space, for about forty people. It was indoor/outdoor carpeting, nothing fluffy, but there was plenty of room to get out of the drizzle, and it is always nice to sleep close to the top of a mountain.

Sunrise at The Palace.

A steady breeze all night blew the clouds and rain somewhere else, and we awoke to a spectacular morning. We felt regal having our breakfast on the deck, looking out at blue skies and a little valley fog. It was the kind of day on which it is perfect to be up high, hiking along a ridge. We were sorry our son hadn't had a morning like this, but at his age a beautiful view wasn't really high on the list of exciting things.

It was one of the best days of the hike, and one of the prettiest parts of the trail. The ridge along the top of the Sugar Bush ski areas, including Cutts Peak, Nancy Hanks Peak, and Lincoln Peak, and ending at 4006-ft.

Mount Abraham, travels just below the treeline for almost five miles. There are glimpses at the view from the top of each peak, with the grand finale at the top of Mount Abraham.

Mount Abraham isn't a ski mountain, and its rock-covered summit, with a 360-degree view, was a surprise to me. I have since met people to whom "Mt. Abe" is affectionately named as one of their favorite places. As we relaxed, got our new bearings, admired the incredible view and glorified in the beauty of the day, it was easy to see why this mountain holds such popularity.

It is always hard to start down from a beautiful peak, especially when the day is still young and the sun is still warm. But the push of the trail, the ever-changing goals

The view north from the upper slopes of Sugarbush Ridge.

of the day, and thoughts about where we would camp that night finally pulled us downward.

The southern side of Mt. Abe is quite steep, and a long hike down. When we arrived at Lincoln Gap we spoke with some day hikers who said Sunset Rock wasn't too far up the other side, and that we might make it there in time to see the sun set. Another birch glen, and a bed of ferns near the top of the next ridge, as well as a beautiful sunset, were the perfect ending to a perfect day on the trail.

8

Midway–Middlebury– Snowberry

Within the Breadloaf Wilderness near Middlebury lies the halfway point between Canada and Massachusetts on the Long Trail. Bill and I took a break at Lake Pleiad, which is just off the trail, to reflect on how far we had come. As Route 25 in Middlebury is just about equidistant from both Route 2 and Route 4, my husband's section of the hike, this was the halfway point for both of us.

One of the advantages of hiking the LT during a relatively rainy summer, besides the easy availability of water, was the incredible lushness of the woods. The ferns were nearly as tall as I; wood sorrel was blooming everywhere. At times it felt almost tropical. Much of the trail, even along the ridges, is wetland. My boots were constantly caked with mud, even though I was careful to use the log and wood walkways that help to preserve the ecosystem. Having spent a fair amount of time hiking in the White Mountains of New Hampshire, where up high means rock, this lushness was a surprise. (They don't call it the Granite State without reason.)

Another pleasant surprise was the increased visibility on the ridges due to the ice storm of January 1998. Having hiked in the Whites, I had wondered if I would feel claustrophobic to be in the woods for almost the whole of the LT. While at the time of the storm the damage was so severe that parts of the trail were closed, by the year 2000 new growth hid some of the scars, but also left holes in the foliage for glimpses of the view. The fire towers and ski areas also helped by affording outstanding views on many peaks. My luck at having clear weather for almost every peak was an incredible gift.

One of the plants I associate with high, northern places is the snowberry. Although considered an alpine species, snowberries are also found near some of my favorite lakes in the north country. These tiny white berries on delicate green foliage have a tangy mint taste that is all their own. For some reason, we found the largest snowberries I have ever seen at Lake Pleiad. They were in a protected spot along the lake, and were a nice addition to our picnic lunch, along with wild blueberries

The quiet waters of Lake Pleaid in the Breadloaf Wilderness.

growing almost out of the rocks. A swim before lunch, relaxing in the sun afterwards, and nibbling on wild fruit were pleasant ways to celebrate our halfway point.

After spending a leisurely lunchtime, we followed the trail up one of the ski slopes of the Middlebury Snow Bowl, another ski area we have visited during the winter. Hiking over ski areas is sometimes unpleasant to purists, who would prefer that the peaks were left in their natural state. Having raised our boys as ski racers, we have spent many a cold morning driving to various mountains to watch our children and their friends come careening down a mountainside.

Before the hike, I remember thinking, "When I hike the Long Trail, I will go over the top of this mountain, and that one, too." Now, having completed the trail, and still attending ski races, I look forward to being near the trail, and remember each mountain from the top as well as the bottom.

Meeting non-hikers at road crossings while hiking was always an interesting experience. First of all, they all seemed so clean. At Smuggler's Notch this was especially noticeable. Many people vacationing in Stowe hike to Sterling Pond for the day. As folks passed me by, it seemed they all wore white, and wafts of shampoo and aftershave drifted behind them on the trail. I wondered what scent drifted behind me.

Many folks we met at road crossings were tourists from other states enjoying the beautiful scenery of Vermont. Many had no idea that tucked in the woods close by was a trail which could take them to Canada or to Massachusetts. Most had heard of the Appalachian Trail, few of the Long Trail. Most assumed that the Long Trail was established after the AT, instead of the other way around. It was fun to give the trail a little publicity.

We met a young family at the base of Mount Abraham, just at dusk, who had hiked a little way up the trail, but were returning before it became dark. They were amazed that we were hiking into the woods at this time of day, with no idea of where we would camp for the night. It was at times like this that I realized I had adopted the culture of the trail, which has its own flow, quite different from that of cars, lights, and television.

As the evening drew near after our pleasant afternoon at Lake Pleiad, and once again the weather was threatening rain, we decided to check out Sucker Brook Shelter. It didn't sound too inviting, but as all the shelters on the LT are close to the trail, it was fun to see them and compare, and make notes of places we would like to revisit.

The trail near Sucker Brook was our first experience of "slabbing" the side of a mountain. In the north, the Long Trail sticks to the ridges. If you look up to the highest point you can see, that is most likely where the trail goes. As we traveled further south, the trail more often followed along the sides of mountains, meaning easier hiking but sometimes less of a view.

When we arrived at the shelter, it was once again crowded. I had passed many empty shelters in the north, but as I traveled south there were more weekend hikers on the trail. A group of over-supplied college students were spending their last night on the trail at Sucker Brook Shelter. They had hoped to meet more young people on the trail, but hadn't, and were ready for more social life, so they were getting off at Middlebury.

At about this point in the hike, Bill was beginning to be concerned about having enough protein. Although my eating was comparatively minimal, most men I met on the trail were constantly hungry. The balance of amount of food, pack weight, and resupply points are major considerations in planning any long distance hike. The young men at Sucker Brook had definitely voted for more food and more weight. Their packs were huge! We had considered hitchhiking into Middlebury for more supplies, but thought we would be O.K. It's a rather long hike from the trail to Middlebury, and for me it was always hard to leave the trail at all.

Trail magic really does happen. One of the college students asked if we wanted any of their supplies. They had enough to get them to Mount Abraham, and since they had decided to cut their hike short they were more than willing to lighten their load. They just happened to have cheese and an extra jar of peanut butter, as well as some protein bars. It was worth bypassing the shelter and setting up in the rain to meet these generous young folks.

As we were getting ready to leave the shelter, having filled our water jugs and replenished our protein supply, a pair of hikers came from the south and said they had just met a mother and baby moose on the trail. It was great to see the young folks so excited about the chance to see one of these amazing animals. A couple of them headed out with their cameras and got a picture. We let them go first, not that we could keep up with pack-less teenagers, anyway. We see moose frequently in our fields, and were happy to give up the chance to these younger hikers.

We camped in the rain on Romance Mountain, once again glad that the tent was small and easy to set up. We were more than halfway on our journey. One more night on the trail and we would be close to the Inn at Long Trail, a mecca for LT and AT hikers.

9

A Day on the Trail and More Trail Magic

The Long Trail is a magical place. The world is a magical place, too, and since completing my hike, whenever something unexpected and wonderful happens, with a little shiver up the spine, I refer to it as trail magic. Sometimes trail magic occurs because of timing, sometimes it happens because of a change in plans, and sometimes there are more concrete examples of random acts of kindness.

Similar incidents of trail magic happened twice on the trail, in different sections, both times while hiking along a brook. At the spot where the trail crossed the brook, someone had dammed up a small section and filled it with cans of soda and ice tea. One spot even had a bag in which to deposit the empties. Thanks go out daily to those thoughtful people, whoever they are.

By this time in the hike, Bill and I had fallen into a pleasant routine. The next two days were typical of many days on the trail. There was a mixture of ridge walk and woods walk, uphill and downhill, and a mixture of sun and rain. We rose early, stretched, ate breakfast, broke camp. As my husband was a faster hiker, he would often move ahead. If people's paces are too different, it is more work than it is worth to try and stay together. Bill is also a very sociable person, so I would often catch up with him as he visited with northbound hikers.

The trail over Mount Horrid was fogged in and drizzling, so we had no view. We met a U.S. Forest Service worker near the road crossing at Brandon Gap, Route 73. She talked about trail washouts and the increased work due to the amount of rain over the summer, especially in southern Vermont. Again I felt fortunate to have hiked in relatively good weather, and that all the major peaks had been clear.

The sun came out at Sunrise Shelter, where we stopped for lunch. Our luck in the weather was reinforced when we met Nolte, who was "hiking for sunshine." He had spent only one day in the sun since leaving Massachusetts, almost two weeks before. I hope he found some sunny peaks up north.

We would often stop at a shelter for lunch. There was

usually a water source, there was always great reading in the trail journal, and the shelters provided a break from the sun, wind or rain. We would sometimes cook soup with cheese melted on top, other times make a meal of trail mix, granola bars, and beef jerky. It was our longest stop of the day, and once in a while we would even take time for a short nap.

More trail magic happened after lunch at Sunrise Shelter. Bill had left his sunglasses on top of Mount Abraham, and the glare was really bothering him when the sun did shine. A woman at the shelter happened to have an extra pair, which she gave him. Random acts of trail magic were becoming common on the trail.

As we hiked the long ridge overlooking Chittenden Reservoir, Bill was in the lead as usual. I saw him up ahead talking to a pair of young hikers, and admiring the view. An exclamation of recognition came from my husband as he realized one of the hikers was a classmate of our son, and a performer in several musical productions in which I had been involved.

He had been away at college, and in trail garb, with long hair and a beard, did look a little different. It was a nice visit, and he highly recommended the Inn at Long Trail. I had seen one other person I knew on the trail, as well as another who would be attending college with a close friend. It really is a small, magical world.

Later on most days, Bill's pace would slow. We would

often take a mid-afternoon break at a lookout spot or near some water. Then we would hike together, discussing whatever was on our minds, or just walking quietly enjoying the sounds of the woods.

Evening is perhaps my favorite time to hike. If you have been hiking all day, by evening the thought of finishing for the day becomes appealing, but also gives a little extra burst of energy. The weather is usually cooler, the birds begin their evening songs, the slanted light is beautiful. We would often hike until nearly dark, just because it was so enjoyable.

When we did stop for the day, finding a comfortable camping spot, one of us would set up the tent while the other lit the stove and started heating water for whatever type of pasta meal was on the menu. The whole process took about 10 minutes. Then dinner and dishes (one pot and two spoons), took about 10 minutes more. The simplicity of it all, of really having everything you needed to do finished in about 20 minutes, was truly a rewarding part of the hike.

We live in a house we built ourselves, as we accumulated the time and money to build it. As all homeowners know, there are always projects to do and nothing is ever finished. On the trail, in the evening after supper, everything was done. We could read, or sit and stare at the view, without a thought about productivity.

Hiking is a relatively inexpensive hobby. Money is

not being made, but little is being spent. The physical benefits are enormous. We were both the strongest we had been in years after finishing the trail. Hiking can be goal-oriented, but it doesn't have to be. The beauty of the woods, the hiker's high from being on top of tall mountains, and the sharing of these events are benefits that really can't be measured.

Perhaps it was our reflective mood, or the time of day, but Wetmore Gap held an incredibly peaceful quality for both of us. Situated between two ridges, it forms a wind tunnel, and by the look of the trees, the wind seldom stops. For both of us, the stunted trees and constant breeze reminded us of the ocean, and held the soothing quality of a day at the beach.

As we neared the Inn at Long Trail, I was excited at the thought of seeing our boys, but suddenly realized that I would miss hiking with my partner. We hadn't spent a week alone together since our children were born, and it had been wonderful to share the time and magic of the mountains together.

Would it be as much fun on my own again? A milder form of the apprehension I felt at the very beginning of the hike resurfaced. I knew I could rely on myself, but it had been nice to have someone to share the load, and the view. Both parts seemed important; the time alone and the time together, and I felt very lucky to have had the chance to experience both types of trail magic.

10

The Inn at Long Trail and Sunset on Killington

Although the Long Trail no longer officially passes the Inn at Long Trail, for several days before we arrived there people were talking about it. "Stop at the Inn!" "Stay if you can, it's worth it!" "Laundry!" "Great breakfast!" "You gotta check it out!!" As we knew there would also be a phone, and it was where we had tentatively arranged for Bill to be picked up, we decided to stay at the Inn.

When we first came out of the woods and met a group of vacationers all dressed in white, and saw the Inn, which looked much more respectable than we did at that moment, we began to reconsider. The Inn is also situated very close to Route 4, and we wondered about the noise of traffic all night. As the weather had finally cleared, and it was a beautiful evening, it was difficult to go inside.

We visited with other hikers on the lawn chairs in front of the Inn, many who were going through the same decision making as we were; some had stayed the night before and were having a hard time leaving. I had been on the trail for two weeks, and the thought of a hot shower grew more inviting all the time.

Although I always kept one set of dry clothing, every pair of socks I had was either wet, or encased with mud, or both. It was probably difficult to tell where the socks ended and my legs began, as I was pretty much coated with mud from the knees down. The difference between the hikers and tourists is pretty clear at the Inn.

My mind was made up to stay, but Bill was vacillating. We went inside to look around, and the smells from the kitchen helped to make up his mind. We decided to check in. The one rule of the Inn is that packs need to be either in your room or outside. "Is it because of the clutter?" we asked. "No, because of the smell!" was the answer.

The Inn is a beautiful partial log structure built into a cliff, literally. A huge piece of rock outcropping is the focal point of both the dining room and the Irish Pub. There is a room with a televison and lots of games—

Saying goodbye at the Inn at Long Trail on Route 4.

board games, not video games. There were no TVs in the rooms, for which I was very thankful. My favorite room, aside from the laundry, which was extremely popular, was a huge living room full of cozy couches, a piano, and a fireplace.

After long, hot showers we did laundry, while enjoying supper in the Irish Pub. "Excellent Guinness!" my husband told everyone. The Long Trail and Appalachian Trail coincide just north of the Inn, so it was our first meeting with folks who had been hiking from

Georgia. It turned out that a group who had been hiking with each other off and on was all meeting for a little party that night at the Inn. Some folks had hiked off the trail to be there for the fun. We listened to stories, sang songs, and enjoyed the company, then fell into a very deep sleep. Our room faced the woods, not the highway. Probably the front rooms have a view, but we were glad for the quiet, and felt incredibly luxurious.

I felt a little guilty the next morning when I heard the torrential rain on the roof. There were many hikers out in their tents dealing with another rainy morning. However, I had no urge to jump back on the trail. We thoroughly enjoyed our breakfast, which was included in the price of the room. Then we called home to arrange for Bill to be picked up. As the rain continued, we enjoyed a lazy morning. We took another shower, read a little, and talked to other hikers.

Bill thought about re-entry into the life of work, transporting kids, tending to the garden and our animals. I thought about another week on the trail, and hiking solo again. It is just about exactly 100 miles from Route 4 to the Massachusetts border. My goal was to hike the rest of the trail in a week. So far I had hiked over 14 miles in a day, but I wasn't sure if I could sustain that pace for seven days in a row.

Both of our children arrived to pick up their father, and it was wonderful to be together again as a family.

We went to the store nearby to restock for the final week, I heard about soccer camp, and saw pictures of our older son's graduation trip to Alaska. I felt rested and physically ready to continue my journey, but the family pull was strong. The rain had stopped, but we lingered over lunch, enjoying each other's company.

Killington looks a long way up from Route 4, and as Vermont's second highest peak, it is. The family drove me to the trail, heading south. As I left them smiling and waving, I did have thoughts of saving the last hundred miles for another year, and jumping into the car with them.

The next few hours on the trail were really the only time I felt a little lonely. The selfishness of taking three weeks out of family life all for myself, picturing my overgrown garden and all the unfinished summer projects, knowing my older son would soon be leaving for college, thus changing our family dynamics—all these thoughts led to a few hours of melancholia.

As I started uphill, a strong wind blew the clouds away, and seemed to clear my head as I climbed. Soon I was back on the trail in spirit as well as in body. The recently relocated Long Trail now bypasses Pico Peak. A young friend had been working on building this new part of the trail earlier in the summer, and I had promised to say hello to her crew leaders if I saw them.

Sure enough, I soon came upon Youth Conservation

Corps workers moving rocks. This wonderful program is open to high school students and young adults who want to work in the woods for a month in the summer. Some groups work at state parks, and others do a variety of tasks to maintain sections of the Long Trail. They really experience what can be accomplished physically by working together as a group, and get paid as well. For some it is a great experience, for others, such as my young friend, it can really be life-changing.

I decided not to take the side trail to Pico, hoping to get to the top of Killington before dark. "It's all downhill after Killington," seasoned LT hikers had assured me. By the time I reached the summit—all alone on the second highest summit in Vermont—my spirits were also elevated. I was so lucky to have such a supportive family. I was so lucky to have had clear weather for every major peak except Camel's Hump. I was so lucky to have the chance to be here in the woods, hiking the entire length of the beautiful state to which my ancestors had migrated from Scotland.

For about a week I had watched Killington get closer and closer, but because of its height couldn't see beyond. Now I had a view of what was to come. Although I grew up in western Massachusetts, I didn't do a lot of hiking as a young person. Camping on top of Mount Monadnock in southern New Hampshire, climbing Mount Greylock in Massachusetts, and a high school outing club trip to the Adirondacks were about the only big hikes of my early years. The southern Vermont mountains of Glastenbury, Stratton, and Bromley were new territory. It was exciting to see them.

It had been an emotional day, and part of me was tempted to spend the night on top of Killington. But I was energized, and ready to get a good start on my goal of 100 miles in a week. I decided to push onward.

About three-quarters of an hour later I met a young man who asked how far it was to the summit, and could I direct him to the water supply. I learned that he was taking his mother (age 60) on her first backpacking trip, and really wanted to watch the sunset with her from the top of Killington. He had hiked ahead to get water, which he was going to take back to her.

He practically jogged ahead, and a short while later he jogged back past me, with water, having left his pack at the shelter so that he could carry his mom's pack. Soon I met them both, and complimented her on an amazing son. I noticed she still wore her pack, and the young man explained that she had refused to give it up. I hope they got to see the sunset, or at least the sunrise the next day. For me the interchange was one more example of trail magic to keep my spirit floating down the trail.

11

Peaks and Lakes

In my opinion, nothing feels better after a day of hiking than diving into some cool water and stretching out for a swim. The Long Trail affords many brooks and streams suitable for a quick dip, but three lakes in southern Vermont are spaced perfectly in between mountains to have a mid-day swim for three days in a row.

The first is Little Rock Pond, a sweet little spot right next to the trail. I arrived in the middle of the day and had the place to myself. After a nice swim and some lunch I spent an hour sunbathing on the rocks. Again, the timing couldn't have been better, because by the time I was close to the summit of Baker Peak later in the day, rain had moved in. I camped for the night, once again letting the steam from my soup warm my tent and myself.

Sometime the next morning I arrived at Griffith Lake, and again was alone by the water. I would always approach ponds and lakes quietly to look for wildlife, especially moose. But although the evidence was everywhere, I never did see one on the trail. The weather was often a bit cloudy during this part of my hike, but I was always warm enough to go for a dip. After my swim, I traveled over Peru Peak, Styles Peak, and then to the top of Bromley Mountain.

Bromley also has a fire tower, which was fogged in when I got there, so I didn't bother climbing it. I went into the ski patrol hut to take a break from the wind and put on another layer for the hike down. Seeing a phone

Little Rock Pond in the Green Mountain National Forest.

on the wall, I picked it up and was surprised to hear a dial tone.

Instinctively I called home collect, and Bill answered. Since it was the middle of a Saturday afternoon, I was amazed that he was home and inside the house. Tentatively I made plans for when I would finish the trail, and asked him to call my sister about trying to meet me. Since my pack and my guidebook were outside, I wasn't exactly sure how much farther I had to go.

After saying goodbye I looked at my book and realized I would need to hike 17–20 miles for the next three days to be out of the woods when I had asked my sister to meet me. Would my legs hold out to keep up that kind of pace? The push to finish was getting stronger, but I was getting tired.

I had always thought of Stratton Mountain as one of the "fancy" ski areas of Vermont, and imagined Stratton Pond a crowded, touristy place. What a nice surprise to find no one at all at the pond, despite signs stating it was a heavy use area.

After finishing a swim and changing back into hiking gear, I was even more surprised to see a canoe paddling towards me. The friendly caretaker said that the canoe had been delivered to him one day; he didn't even have to get it there himself. It looked like a pretty idyllic way to spend the summer.

On the shore of Stratton Pond.

The rain of the summer of 2000 wasn't felt only in Vermont. I had been meeting many Appalachian Trail hikers who felt as though they had been slogging through mud since Georgia. At Stratton Pond I met a young couple who seemed oblivious to any sort of problems, leastwise the weather.

The young man's eyes lit up at the sight of the water, and he immediately pulled a fishing rod out of his pack. He questioned the caretaker about his chances of catching anything, and despite a slightly discouraging prospect, began to cast happily. When I inquired about their favorite part of the AT, they proceeded to tell me about many wonderful places with a youthful enthusiasm that was very infectious and refreshing. The stories kept pouring out, and it was evident that they had made the most of their experience.

For about a week I had been hearing about and reading in the shelter journals about the hiker "condo" on top of Stratton Mountain. The ski patrol house, which was open to hikers, was equipped with a television, flush toilets, and a washing machine. It was rumored that some hikers never went any further. Another event at Stratton was a huge all-you-can-eat buffet at the bottom of the gondola, with a free ride down and back up for hikers.

One couple had a sad tale about their stop at Stratton. They had heard about and looked forward to the meal. (Many people I met on the trail were constantly hungry.) They had decided to stay at the "condo," so left their packs, and rode down on the gondola. Sadly, they missed the last serving of the buffet, and by the time they found somewhere else to get food, also missed the last gondola ride back up the mountain. They had no buffet and had to hike an extra mountain to get back where they started.

By this time in my hike I was eating small amounts frequently, intermittently snacking when I felt the need. Cereal in the morning, some protein mid-morning, dried fruit in the afternoon, pasta in the evening. I knew I would do no justice to a big buffet. I considered riding the gondola for another cup of Green Mountain Coffee, as well as the fun of the ride, and the change of pace. When I arrived at the top of the mountain, and climbed the fire tower to look into the fog, I was told that the gondola was another mile down a side trail.

A very nice woman, who lived in the fire tower house, said that I could leave my pack with her, and also that there was a snack shop at the top of the gondola with Green Mountain Coffee. She also warned me that the gondola would shut down if there was any lightning, which looked like a possibility.

Feeling weightless without my pack, I set off at a bit of a jog out the side trail. The "condo" was plush, but I was very glad I had been warned about the gondola and lightning. After visiting with the snack shop attendant and heading out with my coffee, I noticed the small crowd of tourists all heading towards the gondola. The threat of thunderstorms had once again forced its closing.

I easily could have been stuck at the bottom of the mountain with a long hike ahead. Instead, I carefully carried my Green Mountain Coffee cup for the rest of the afternoon, savoring it sip by sip. It seemed a little silly to have walked two miles for a cup of coffee, but all sorts of things begin to make sense when you are by yourself for extended time out in the woods.

12

A Day for the Dogs

It really wasn't all bad, although for many reasons the next-to-last-can't-wait-to-be-finished was the worst of my 23 days on the trail. It is interesting how much the ideas of good and bad can be affected by weather when you have been in the woods for a while. I saw a few glimpses of the sun in the morning, then the clouds became mist, and then became a foggy, gloomy, steady rain.

My thoughts about seeing the Holyoke Range, a landmark of my growing up years, from the top of Glastenbury Mountain faded quickly into the fog. Many hikers have philosophies to keep them going on rainy days: "You either sweat or you're wet, what's the difference?" "It's cooler!" "No need to take side trails to look at views, so you make better time." "You have two choices, you can either keep walking or you can sit in a shelter and watch the rain."

I had become an experienced rainy day hiker. Since my first deluge on Mount Mansfield, I had traveled quite a few miles in a raincoat. At this point in my hike the urge to finish was getting stronger every minute. I had pushed myself the last week, and was close to achieving my goal of 100 miles in seven days. In the few days since I had called Bill from the top of Bromley, I had hiked close to 20 miles a day, and I was getting tired.

Someone might be waiting for me in Massachusetts the next evening. Someone might hike in to try and meet me. Would someone be there? Would I be there? Although by this time I was a firm believer in trail magic, and was optimistic that something would work out, I didn't have any way of knowing for sure. Would my legs hold out for two more long days?

It was still over 30 miles to the border, and then there was the walk on the Massachusetts side to the trailhead. The rain continued. This wasn't a shower, it was a steady rain. My Gore-Tex coat and boots no longer kept me dry. Saturated socks pull the water right down into your boots, and I understood why people wore gaiters around their calves and over their boots. I used to think gaiters were just for cross-country skiing.

A raw wind was blowing the rain sideways. I saw no one all morning, except some sleeping hikers who had pitched their tent inside of Caughnawaga Shelter. They were probably either sick of packing up a wet tent or sick of the bugs, or both. It was dreary, monotonous hiking.

Glastenbury Mountain, although tree-covered, has a fire tower on top, and folks tell me it's a wonderful view. As I approached the tower, I was startled to hear voices, and looked up to see two hikers coaxing their canine companion down the open metal stairs. I felt sorry for the dog. His people made the choice to be out on a mountain in the rain. The pooch sure perked up when his feet hit solid ground again.

As they hiked on, I, too, climbed the tower, although they had assured me everything was fogged in. Habit, I guess, or maybe just the change of pace, made me go all the way to the top. The hikers were right. I didn't stay long, and was glad to be headed down the backside of my last big peak. The rain was still steady, but the wind abated a little as I moved down the mountain. I stopped at Goddard Shelter for lunch, and was tempted to stay for awhile, but the rain obviously wasn't going to stop and the movement kept me warm.

My tentative goal was to reach Route 9, the last east/west highway crossing the Long Trail. It would mean another 20-mile day, and still leave 17 miles to be in Williamstown, Massachusetts, the following evening, but I was ready to go home. So on I slogged through

"Vermud," one of Vermont's LT nicknames during the summer of 2000.

Nearing the base of Glastenbury Mountain, I looked up to see another canine hiker complete with a backpack. He looked as bedraggled as I felt. Seeing no sign of his owner, I stopped to chat and explained to him that I planned to be out of the woods the next day, with a roof over my head. When I asked if he would like to come with me, he immediately turned around and followed me down the trail

We soon met his soggy AT thru-hiker companion, who said the thought of several more weeks on the trail seemed far too long on days like this. We all tried to remember why we were out here in the first place, then we headed in opposite directions. I could almost hear the pooch sigh as he turned and followed his master back uphill.

The rain went on and on, the day went on and on, and so did the trail. Where was Route 9, anyway? It started to get dark, and I was feeling a little depressed about not making it to the road crossing. It meant more miles the next day if I was going to finish, and I was exhausted.

Resigning to the end of the day, I began to look for somewhere to pitch my tent. As my tent was very small, and self-standing, it could fit in almost anywhere. There were only a few places on the whole Long Trail that I felt were really unsuitable for camping. The northern side of Route 9, unfortunately, was one of those places.

It is incredibly steep, or at least seemed so in my state of exhaustion. More than that, however, was the fact that there were full-length logs strewn everywhere. It looked as though someone had logged uphill in the winter, but for some reason had been unable to get the logs out. The spring runoff must have produced a log slide.

It was getting darker, and I was now climbing over logs that were almost as tall as I was, scattered like pick-up sticks. Mercifully the rain had stopped, and the breeze felt as though it was blowing in some drier air. I still hadn't found a spot to put up my tent.

After hearing the sound of running water getting louder for quite some time, suddenly there was another sound mixed in. A truck, grinding its way up Route 9! In the fading daylight I saw truck lights, the river, and a beautiful flat campsite, all at the same time. I broke my rule of not camping at any road crossings as a safety precaution. My tent was up, my supper cooked, and I was asleep within a half hour. I had made my goal; the worst day was over.

13

Massachusetts

The uphill hike going south from Route 9 on the Long Trail is as steep on the way up to the ridge as it is on the way down to the highway, but it is amazing what a good night's sleep and a sunny morning can do for one's attitude. There were mixed feelings of "Today I will be finished!" and "It's hard to imagine leaving all this!"

I would be glad to put on dry clothing, anyway, I thought as I donned my still wet outfit from the day before. My rule had been to always keep one set of dry clothing to put on at the end of the day. Since this was probably my last day, I was tempted to keep my dry outfit on, but the woods were wet and I would be soaked quickly, anyway. Besides, I wasn't absolutely sure I would be out of the woods that night. So on with the soggy shorts, glad for the sun to slowly dry everything out.

"But the ending always comes at last; endings always come too fast. They come too fast, but they pass too slow." This is the song line, by Art Garfunkel, that kept going through my head on the final day. Wanting to finish, but not wanting all this to end. Endings always involve a bit of melancholy, but also mean new beginnings. As my dance teacher Bill Evans wrote, "Life is change, and the opportunity to travel the journey of life-long change is a precious gift." My journey on the trail was a gift, and its ending would bring chances for more changes, and more travels on the journey of life.

However, there were still 17 miles to hike before I could settle into a reflective state. The push of the last few days, hiking my longest distances of the trail, was beginning to catch up with me. I felt rugged, but knew it was nearing time for a break. The urge to finish was strong, but I would be tired when I stopped.

I wondered if anyone would be at the end of the trail to meet me. Trail arrangements being what they are, there was really no way of knowing. It didn't really matter, either. My whole family lives within an hour of the Massachusetts end of the trail, so a phone call if it wasn't too late would roust someone to meet me.

One of my diversions while hiking the trail had been singing. I love to sing, and know a lot of songs. Sometimes I would try to remember all the songs from a particular musical, in order. The rhythm of hiking can fit into all kinds of music. Sometimes I would sing out loud; sometimes I'd sing to myself.

On the last day I heard another trail singer as I walked. Many times it was startling to look up and see another hiker close by, especially when I was by myself. Hikers are generally quiet, and often looking down. I'm sure the trail singer I met was surprised when he looked up and saw me. I had stopped to let him pass by, as he was hiking up. This was a common courtesy observed by most hikers. Uphill hikers have the right of way.

After confessing that I, too, was a trail singer, we had a good laugh and discussion about which type of song flowed best with which pace of hiking. I then told him that my sister was meeting me soon. I laughed at myself when I said this because I really had no idea if she was even available to pick me up on this, the designated day. Having stated that she would be there with such confidence made me wonder if it was true, or just wishful thinking.

I hoped that there would at least be another hiker around when I reached the Massachusetts border to take my picture. The disposable camera I brought didn't have any kind of timer to take pictures of myself. (Actually my son and his girlfriend recently took some great pictures of themselves by holding a disposable camera

Reaching the Vermont-Massachusetts border,
270 miles from the starting point.

at arm's length. It really works!) Disposable cameras are lightweight, and you don't have to worry about them. Mine was kept in a plastic bag, and it took some good shots.

Shortly after conversing with the trail singer, another canine hiker approached. She was much happier than the two I had met the previous day in the rain. Something was familiar about this pooch, and I looked up to see my sister following her dog up the trail! The dog had been a puppy the last time I had seen her, and now had her full growth and puppy energy.

Even with the knowledge that my sister is an early riser, I thought she must have camped somewhere the night before. It was still early in the day, and I figured there were still eight or so miles left on the trail. She sure caught the early bird worm that morning. She left home and drove an hour and still was on the trail before me.

In many ways this connection with Massachusetts was the first ending of my hike. Relief mixed again with melancholy, but it was great to have company and extra treats at lunch time. We stopped and ate by Sucker Pond, a pretty spot with an unappealing name. My sister brought fresh fruit—no more raisins! That plum tasted absolutely delightful. Aside from a few blackberries, blueberries and snowberries, and the wild strawberries on top of Jay Peak, my fruit diet had been mostly of the dried variety.

The time, the miles, and the afternoon passed quickly as we caught up on family news and stories of my hike. All of a sudden we were there. The Vermont-Massachusetts state line. Visually it isn't as dramatic as the northern border, but after hiking 270 miles it sure was a welcome sight. Again there were the mixed emotions, along with a celebratory libation and a photo shoot. It was hard to believe I was finished.

This was the second ending, but it was still over three miles to the parking lot where my sister's truck was waiting. Although the weather stayed clear and we had some views, that last stretch seemed to take forever. Endings come too fast and pass too slow. I was finished, but not quite.

We had been hiking since early morning, and the sun was now sinking. Even the energy of our youthful canine companion was beginning to fade. I had been doing this for three weeks, and was amazed that my sister wasn't any more tired than I was. The last of the sun disappeared as we hiked the final stretch down to Williamstown.

Another ending. There was the yellow truck. I could finally take off my boots, which I did immediately. I thought of the barefoot girls and how good their feet had looked at the end of their hike. Mine looked red, shriveled and sore. As I studied my feet, I heard my sister say that she couldn't find the key to the truck. It was too late

Signing off at the border.

in the day to joke. Life seemed surreal for a few minutes. The hike had begun with a lost guidebook and was ending with a lost key?

Thoughts of putting my boots back on and walking the extra mile into town were just about more than I could imagine. I realized at that moment that I was really finished. Really, really finished—no more hiking for a long time. I was ready to travel in motored vehicles for a while. "ALL DONE!" as my son as a two-year-old would scream when he had had enough of a particular situation.

I would have easily regressed to two-year-old tactics if

it could have helped the situation. Screaming didn't seem out of the question. But what was my sister saying from the other side of the truck? She found them?! The door opened in front of me as I looked up from the grassy spot on which I had collapsed. I was really all done.

14

Re-entry

My sister and I drove into Williamstown and stopped at a mini-mart to call Bill and my parents. Then, in a wave of total exhaustion, I had to sit on the curb with my head between my knees for a minute while my sister went inside for juice.

Was this a reaction to the relief of being finished, or exhaustion, or just the stimulation of cars, lights, noise, signs and smells all at once? Who knows? The nausea passed, and the supper we bought for the ride tasted great.

A full moon lit the mountains alongside Route 2, the Mohawk Trail, as we drove to my folks' house, where a shower and bed awaited. My parents live on the edge of the woods in a small town, so the sound of crickets sung me to sleep through the wide open window. It was a different sound than the evening birds on the trail, but just as soothing.

Bill picked me up early the next morning, and we drove in three hours what had taken me three weeks to hike. It was wonderful to be home, in my house in the woods. It was especially good to eat fresh food from my overgrown, but still productive garden.

Celebrations were in order, of course. Songs were written acknowledging my safe return. A PhD certificate—Professional Hiking Degree—was designed for me by an Appalachian Trail hiker. It hangs on my wall beside the official certificate awarded by the Green Mountain Club. Any hiker who has completed the trail, in one trip or many, and completes a journal describing the hike, is given a number. My number is 2000-70-2475, signifying that in the year 2000, I was the 70th person to complete the trail, and the 2,475th person to do so since the trail was created.

It took some time to readjust and revive my energy. The contentment of fulfilling this 20-year goal can't be overstated. My body felt as strong as it had 20 years before. Soon after the end of my hike, Backpacker Magazine published an article listing the 10 best long distance hiking trails in the country. The Long Trail wasn't No. 1, but it was on the list, and it gave me nine other trails to think about and plan for, maybe, someday.

At that moment, however, I was perfectly satisfied to sit on my porch swing, with my feet up, and relive my hike through the Green Mountains of Vermont.

AFTERWORD

The Long Trail and the Green Mountain Club began in 1910 as the vision of James Taylor, a teacher from Saxtons River, Vermont. The stamina and strength of this first president of an amazing group of volunteers is the story of a true pioneer. The numerous obstacles involved in building a footpath all along the ridge of the Green Mountains were merely challenges to be met, so that the ultimate goal could be achieved.

Accomplishing that goal took twenty years and many volunteers, but in 1930 the Long Trail was completed; it was the first long distance hiking trail in the country, extending from one end of Vermont to the other. The Appalachian Trail, which began construction in the 1920s, was not completed until 1937. The Appalachian Trail Conference (longtime overseers of the 2160-mile footpath from Georgia to Maine) utilized the southern end of the Long Trail to connect Massachusetts to the White Mountains of New Hampshire. Thus the Long Trail and the Appalachian Trail coincide for 100 miles, from the Massachusetts border to just north of Route 4 near Killington, Vermont. There, the Appalachian Trail turns to the east and eventually crosses the Connecticut River at Hanover, New Hampshire.

Green Mountain Adventure, an illustrated history of the Long Trail and the Green Mountain Club, written by Jane and Will Curtis and Frank Lieberman, is a thorough and fascinating book describing the process of building the Long Trail. It includes numerous photographs of the trail during its beginning stages, and brings to life the amount of work and energy involved in pursuing this project.

The Green Mountain Club has always relied on volunteers, and continues to do so today. The Long Trail is divided into twelve sections, and individuals may join the GMC as members of one of these particular sections (i.e., as "Section" members) or as "at large" members. All members are invited to help where needed in actual trail work or by contributing funds toward ongoing trail maintenance.

Shelters on the Long Trail (most maintained by GMC) are spaced approximately a day's hike apart all along the trail and vary in construction from primitive lean-to shelters to camps with windows, bunks and tables. Most are named for people who contributed time, energy, and inspiration towards the building and ongoing maintenance of the trail. To join GMC or to obtain more information about the club, write to: The Green Mountain Club, Inc. Route 100, R.R. 1, Box 650, Waterbury Center, VT 05677 or visit their website at www.greenmountainclub.org.

The names of all who have hiked the entire trail have been recorded, beginning with Irving Appleby of Roxbury, Massachusetts, who hiked from Jay Peak to the Massachusetts border in 1926, four years before the actual completion of the trail! Personally inspiring is the second group of recorded end-to-enders—three women, known as the Three Musketeers, who hiked the trail shortly after Appleby.

People love mountains for many reasons. For nearly 100 years the Green Mountain Club has made the Long Trail available to satisfy the longing to be up high; gazing at the vistas, following clear waters, viewing wildlife, and walking through the Green Mountains of Vermont.